Honey in My Hair

poems by

Livia Meneghin

Finishing Line Press
Georgetown, Kentucky

Honey in My Hair

Copyright © 2018 by Livia Meneghin
ISBN 978-1-63534-466-0 First Edition
All rights reserved under International and Pan-American Copyright Conventions.
No part of this book may be reproduced in any manner whatsoever without written permission from the publisher, except in the case of brief quotations embodied in critical articles and reviews.

ACKNOWLEDGMENTS

I would like to express my sincere gratitude to Finishing Line Press, Leah Maines, and the entire editorial staff for making this book—this dream—possible.

I extend regards and much appreciation to those who read my work. This includes Carolyn Forché, my workshop class in Greece, as well as Diana Clark, Jenny Currier, Arielle Lipset, Katie Machen, Keiran Miller, Deirdre Scanlon, Katie Urbanski, and Leah Vitello. Also, Erik Anderson, Meg Day, Joanna Eleftheriou, Sands Hall, Kelly McMasters, and Marci Nelligan.

To my mother, sister, and grandparents for reading, as well as their constant support and love. And to anyone who has believed in me, encouraged me to keep writing. I thank you with my whole heart, and then some.

My trip to Greece would not have been realized if Christopher Bakken had not visited Franklin & Marshall College, so I thank him for taking the time to tell me about WWIG.

I would also like to thank everyone who donated to my GoFundMe campaign, including professors, relatives, and friends; their help further allowed me to enjoy this life-changing ex,perience that has inspired this collection.

Publisher: Leah Maines
Editor: Christen Kincaid
Cover Art: Livia Meneghin
Author Photo: Emily Meneghin
Cover Design: Elizabeth Maines McCleavy

Printed in the USA on acid-free paper.
Order online: www.finishinglinepress.com
also available on amazon.com

Author inquiries and mail orders:
Finishing Line Press
P. O. Box 1626
Georgetown, Kentucky 40324
U. S. A.

Table of Contents

Mármaros 1
Courage 2
Artemis, the Stray 3
IMG_609 – IMG_615 4
Marvels 5
Saint Friday 6
Islands 7
Five More Days 8
I Met an Egyptian Last Night 9
fear 10
Freedom 11
To Ia in 1993 12
Ichtys 13
My Dears 14
The Greatest Crime 15
Letter to Mom, Erasure 16
Octopus Salad 17
Light 19
Storm 20
Notes on Discovery, in Color 21
Slow, Slow 22
Wings 23
Upstairs 24
Her Last Day 25

"None of us understand what we're doing, but we do beautiful things anyway."

—Allen Ginsberg

Mármaros

       know the marble
       know the quiet
Taj Mahal and roses
crossed over canes
       know Clio, goddess
of history carved
in shining stone
       know the refined
taste of tradition
       know there is
Tuckahoe marble
in the Vatican
in Laocoön's battle
with his two sons
against the snake's
bite, a portrait
of human agony
       know I swam out
a metamorphism
through navy
through royal blue
through teal
all for unpolished white
I found the quiet there
sitting atop marble
all around and over
interlocking
crystals and the sea
       know that marble
looks like seashells
when making strides
with incoming waves
and I heard fishermen
say *it will storm*
tomorrow

Courage

The leaves glowed exceedingly green
the day grief was outmuscled
by the sea. And you, the last
person to ever come to a conclusion
about the beauty of stillness,
marveled at their courage. Only
you can see how simultaneously
sacred and wild the clouds are.

And the sea.

And you.

So close to tasting the thyme,
to knowing whether or not Heaven exists,
you are among life. Every morning, you
see stars out your window.
You are near God, and green,
and the sea, and the end, and you don't know.

Artemis, The Stray

       stalks cautiously
on the gravel, each step
strained and stinging,
like the essence of lemon.
She, white

with reptilian eyes,
is wounded.
Still she hunts,
my God, she must.
Under the moon each night,

but no longer in the wildlands,
she weaves through table legs;
the restaurant is nothing
without her, and without us
so is she.

IMG_609 – IMG_615

      I'll take you to the pine tree, honey,
and we'll absorb like clouds in a river.

      I know I did when I met eyes
with the white cat's Egyptian gaze.

      I fell into the deep sea, Aegean glass,
saw the feline and the surface rocks from below.

      Cup your hands, honey,
and let the sea write you a letter.

      Use the color of that lily—so Godgifted
yellow—as ink to write a reply.

      I prefer letters, can't you tell?
I still need to take a picture of that lily.

      I took one of an octopus in Thessaloniki.
I took one of a fish's gills outside its body—

      once inside and filling
now spilling blood on the floor of Aliki.

      See the cook filling
his hands with sea to wash.

      Take me to Mount Athos
so together we can determine whether

      the white in my sky
is a striation of clouds mirroring marble

      or the faraway remnants of a river
dotted on each side by invisible pines.

Marvels

all is well all is well
i tell myself
> but my heart won't stop
> following the beautiful things

i find solar systems in cacti needles
and always comb through
> the grass
> the thyme

she asked me for my lemon at dinner
she sleeps without the covers on
> she's a young woman
> but also a marvel

i want to carve our names in a tree
but for a month i was surrounded
> by pines
> and forgot how to spell

too busy seeing urchins under seaglass
and pouring honey in my hair
> *we just look forward*
> *to the next thing* she says

she is just a girl
for a second she's the universe
> and i'm just a girl
> a clock

with hands that want
to mark
> and watch
> and keep

Saint Friday

I almost dropped my grandmother's engagement ring in the toilet
    but I didn't, thank the saints.
    She said, *You know, it's been through quite a lot anyway.*

I could barely enter Agia Paraskevi because of the incense,
    but I wanted to. I waited until after the service,
    standing in the doorframe and watching the icons
        watch me.

I didn't ask to go fishing with the poet until much later in the day than I planned.
    But we'll still go on Friday.
    There might be a lot of sea, he said.

I haven't tasted the stuffed peppers because I've never liked them.
    But maybe I just dislike American peppers.
    There has to be some Greek food I don't like. No,
        everything edible here
        is holy. I know
        by the way
        Saint Friday seems to nod
        in her portrait at our table.

Islands

try to sign the seaglassblue
of the Aegean in ASL

your hands
        your words

you will fail

take me to Taormina instead
take me back through

the haze
        to the haze

and lose me

to the Mediterranean medusa
and the Sicilian sunburn

your fists
        your cheekbones

can't help but touch

the cliffs of Thassos
the cool marble

you will soon be released
        from those days

marooned in Aliki

Five More Days

I'm getting impatient.
I want to roll my tongue
around the sounds:

silver and green
cucumbers and conversation
coffee tables and the sea.

I don't like the way
Five more days
sounds. A trumpet
that falls from the trellis
and into my soup,
         her wine glass.

I Met an Egyptian Last Night

I had two silver
bands, though neither from a lover.

My fingers swelled
and my eyes fell
and my mouth was uncomfortable
    open or closed.

This morning my yogurt
was loosened by the honey. My jaw
too, and I sang under my breath:
    things are falling apart.

Last night, I met her. Humidity
in the air as she watched me eat
watermelon and honeydew. I tried
to avoid her attention, but

I couldn't think of a reason why.

fear

there is fear and there
is everything
especially when there is a lot of sea
you just need to decide where
you want to be
when even the light is scared

Freedom
—for Ιωαννα Ελευθεριου, previously published in the Franklin & Marshall College Alumni Arts Review

    is a woman
from *Κύπρος*. She can swim
the *Αιγαίο*, smell
the pine of *Θασος* in her hair,
and still remember

    her father.
When sailboats look
like seagulls, she still
dances the *ζεϊμπέκικο* better
than any man because

    she understands
what a cage is. Freedom held
my face and said, *You have so much
power; you have nothing to fear.*
She looked into my eyes

    with *διαχρονική αγάπη,*
an eternal love that wrinkled her tanned skin.
She kissed my cheek and stroked
my hair, she knew I was crying
on the inside.

    λένε όχι στο φόβο,
cried the Greek people in the streets
of *Θεσσαλονίκη*. *Say no to fear.*
Freedom walks within the crowds,
within the wounds.

To Ia in 1993

> *I said, "I'm afraid of not existing."*
> *"Millions and billions of years you did not exist—what was the problem?"*
> *"But now I've formed relationships," I said.*
> - Rachel Aviv

You won't see anything
when you look out,

        so look up—
there will be hundreds of stars.

I'm not so sure what to make
of the sea and today

        a woman told me
        pineapples grow in her yard

        and another took fallen flowers
        off the ground and

        put them where her buttons
        should go

        and the whitecrested navy
        raced marble tested by thousands

        of years
        of existence

but I think I know the night
here. Look.

You will see and be
everything.

Ichthys

I am not powerful. I still carry you
in my heart when I know I shouldn't,
when I told myself I should stop.

I tasted octopus and wine
asking questions afterward;
I climbed a mountain not knowing
how high I would travel. How

you'd fallen in love
and I wounded me.
I want to intersect my arms
and have you in between.

On my wrist I wear *Ichtys*
next to a goldplated arrow.
The one-eyed fish wards off
enemy emotions and the arrow shoots on sight.

My Dears

ladies dancing the *hasakipo*,
    and singing along to
    lyrics learned two days before
    about a woman with the moon in her hair
that old man moving his hips
    embodying all ages at once
the fisher-poet sitting in his chair,
    surrounded by men, cigarette smoke,
    empty glasses, grins, and poker chips for later
an Italian from the town where I was born
an Italian couple who wear yellow caps
    and, despite their age, aren't afraid to dance
the Italian man who drives me to a lagoon, talking
    about Chomsky and how the world could be better

(This is one night. And every night.)

a girl who teaches me ASL and asks me
    how to say *thank you* in Greek
a friend who loves hugs and says sorry too much,
    who fell in love with her first bite of a Greek peach
handwritten letters
    and other things no one reads
    anymore
honey on yogurt, spilling slowly off my spoon,
    complimenting peaches picked
    just minutes before
a praying mantis alongside the dirt path
    to a neighbor's house
the trumpet flowers providing shade
    during the heat of the late morning

The Greatest Crime

       is talking to yourself and not writing it down
the white and you
Limenas lemons and cats running up trees
a *papagallo* and a soldier light on his feet
sea urchins and sleeping atop marble

       is picking soon-to-be pesto and fishing with a poet
sea salt on skin and sunlight on shells
               a lonely corn poppy in the quarry
               years of yellow-centered anemones
               brugmansia too perfect for behind girls' ears

       is eating sea urchins and swimming farther out than ever before
superheroines and circle dances
the wind and grape-filled trellises
καλινικτα and *buona sera*
a soft χαρμολυπη before the wound

Letter To Mom, Erasure

          I
am feeling   what
            other people

miss   . I'm
going   . I'm
worried
    crashing.
              writing.

            I'm hiding
behind my   becoming
        again.
  I'm

    wrong and I can't

      see

Octopus Salad

Yield: 8 servings
Active time: 20 minutes
Total time: 2 hours (or if you can, years)

Ingredients:
    1 octopus, not too young (they deserve the sea too much)
    1/3 cup parsley from the Archondissa veranda (ask first)
    3 garlic cloves, finely chopped
    X memories, as many as you'd like
    1 celery rib, remember Eve and your female ancestors as it's halved lengthwise and thinly sliced crosswise
    1 carrot, I would tell you to cut it the same way as the celery, but we all know you are busy, so do as you please; we're only making salad
    ¼ cup of olive oil from Taso's land (one rifle shot to signal your presence, two for your leaving)
    ¼ cup of fresh lemon juice, from Kyria Eva's kitchen or the home Stamatis built; he has lemon trees
    ½ teaspoon of fine (Aegean) sea salt
    ¼ teaspoon of dried oregano

Preparation:
Hunt for octopus. Once caught, hit delicious darling on a rock 40 times. Yes, it must be this way, like when I was five years old and I would say to everyone in the supermarket, "Guess how old my mom is? She's forty!"

Dissect and disassemble octopus, discarding the head and dicing the tentacles.

Submerge the octopus in water and gently simmer, until tender, pot uncovered, for 40 minutes to 1 hour. Try not to look at the beast; start to think of her as food and not alive earlier that morning.

My mom craved octopus salad when she was pregnant with me—that, and *parmigiano*. The cheese made me smart and the octopus gave me a soul.

Drain and cool to room temperature. In a new bowl, add ingredients, like friends. Additional sea salt is always welcome, since you'll have to leave Aliki soon. Let it stand 30 minutes for ~~feelings~~ flavors to develop.

Light

Light blue is not the color
of truth. Rub aloe on your wounds,
worldly and not,
and try to touch the sky again.

Light green is not the color
of the sea. And yet you love to dive.
Look in the mirror; look at my eyes.

Light red is not what it says.
There is something incredibly angular
about rubies, and the way
they feel when they fall out of your mouth.

Light is the belief
there is something else
besides darkness.

Light is what you see
when you are

already happy.

Storm

How dare my bones find
Arctic in Aegean,
my view dipped in navy
so all I can see is the wind
as rows of shadows
pull the shore farther
away from here.

We are sitting on the patio
      (where last night
         we listened to a trembling
         and the water and the whiskey and a story)
talking about a tragedy in Charleston.
The sea reveals stretch marks and cold crests…
The marble doesn't want to speak.

At the other end of the restaurant
the fisherman and his friends
are conversing like storm clouds,
their Greek rolling and building,
grayer and grayer. I know
they are talking about ATM's
the way we are talking about guns.

I hope the lavender
of the distant sky
will send the sea home
soon. But there is
no answer,
no color,
no weather.

Notes on Discovery, In Color

to•mor•row |tə'môrō; -'märō|
noun
the day commencing at midnight; (more simply) the day after today; (less simply) where a piece of my mind, no matter what I am doing, always lives. On good days that house is large and filled with light and the light makes colors like forest and peach and espresso.

* * *

Tell yourself the crashing of stones feels like the color of waves and wine on the inside. Write in the grainy sand, with your toe, I do not fear it: I have been there and pretend the olive tree you sit under is an elm. Think of Sylvia Plath when you hear the waves and the laughter of inebriation; try to decide which one is more constant.

* * *

Think of the singing yellow of lemon we find so
refreshing on calamari. I am always in awe at the person towards the other end of the table who could bite into one, and on a good day, swallow.

* * *

I placed my forearm up against the wall last night.
My skin seeming so tan on the white for a while,
until I witnessed the blueness of my veins.

* * *

Did you know my eyes change color?
Sometimes they are two sunlit grape vine leaves.
        Otherwise they're orchards, guarded by a ring of brown
        still allowing you to taste the fruit.

Slow, Slow

She saw fallen pinecones,
nestled and nested in needles,
browned by the sun
            or their age.

Short of breath, she noticed
her stomach and her heart had switched places.
Slow, slow, said the Baha'i man,
though she's always wanted to be gone.

Later, she takes a nap on her balcony,
her thoughts unify and her body lies
surrounded by yellow walls and the sea.
She dreams of the world spilling

from her mouth like the nectar—
like the splendor—of the peach she ate
up in the mountains with him.
Fruit sweeter than the *tsipouro* or the truth

they swallowed. Her ears consider
the quiet conversation of marble
and the shy hello of the Aegean
down by the beach. His voice lingers

still, balancing ancient stone and sea.
With eyes closed, she remembers
the crunch under her feet as they hiked higher,
looking for something bigger than time.

Slow, slow, says the κοπελα
to herself on the sunset-drenched balcony,
when she reaches her pride
and realizes she can be swallowed too.

Wings

"There must be wind,"
he told me
in a voice sounding
quite like my own.
"Only then can you witness
the wingspan of the sea."

The Aegean is old,
I thought as I traced
my fingertips along its surface.
I closed my eyes,
each current oscillating
under my young body.

My wings, the wind,
and the water pulled me
both away from all I've ever known
and towards him. I looked
into the Thassian's eyes
and there was an understanding.

Upstairs

See the man writing poetry on cigarettes
and the octopus soaked in wine.
The marble's mouth widens
when the sea is no longer
glass, but the deaf can't tell
if stone screams or yawns.

Hear the vendor say, *God must be Greek,*
and believe him—if you can.

See the large white cat,
the one with paws like a lion's,
stalking the veranda,
ensuring that no other feline finds
a single scrap.
But he is wounded.

Something far away
from where the pinecones built
nests in the fallen needles
had to have given him that bad ear.
He twists it around at the sound
of the tide and our swallowing.

Your stomach is where your heart should be
and your heart fell downstairs;

I know, I've seen this before.
Think. Your heart was so heavy,
saturated in saltwater and poetry,
in God and your own wounds.
Try to see and hear
the wonders of upstairs instead.

Her Last Day

         is a kaleidoscope
of salt and water and fear.
She holds

kalos, beauty,

tentacles clinging to her cupped fingers,
and desperation to stay soaked,
all in the form of a young octopus.

Eidos, form.

In her hands she sees shards
of Italy and New York
and her three-year old self

getting swallowed by a wave
on a beach she doesn't remember...
her first memory,

or a dream.
Something she mustn't spend
too much time looking into,

Skopeô, to look to.

She looks to the horizon;
seaglass meets sky.
Time catches up to her.

She bends down
and lets the young octopus
go.

Livia Meneghin is a poet, essayist, and artist with a BA in English-Creative Writing from Franklin & Marshall College. *Honey in My Hair* is her first chapbook publication, and was a finalist in the Atlas Review's 2016 Chapbook Competition. Her poem, "Freedom," was originally published in the *F&M Alumni Arts Review*. The collection was inspired by her time on the island of Thassos with Writing Workshops in Greece. There she fell in love with honey, marble, a small stray cat, and of course, the sea.

She is currently working on three novel projects and a full book of poems. Under the guidance of Carolyn Forché and Katie Ford in poetry workshops, as well as in conversation with Andrea Gibson and Franny Choi, Livia has absorbed invaluable writerly advice as a student and now has molded her own voice in this first collection. Previously she has shadowed Ansel Elkins in F&M's Emerging Writers Festival; there she experienced firsthand the value of a supportive writing community. Her essays can be found on her blog, liviameneghin.wordpress.com, as well as HandwrittenWork.com. She has lived in Italy, Greece, England, New York, and Pennsylvania, though currently resides in Massachusetts.

www.ingramcontent.com/pod-product-compliance
Lightning Source LLC
LaVergne TN
LVHW041516070426
835507LV00012B/1608